THE IRISH WOLFHOUND GUIDE

The Irish Wolfhound Guide

ALFRED W. DeQUOY

1977

Second Edition

Author's Note

The reader is asked to note with care the title of this book and to remember throughout its reading that it is only a "guide". There are very few matters about which one can be dogmatic. In this work on the Irish Wolfhound, apart from my own comments and analyses, the divergent views of many people, published since 1879, are given. The reader is provided with all the evidence for the exercise of his own judgment.

As for the organization of the book, I have assumed that the reader has just become acquainted with the breed. He first wishes to be given a general history of the breed, then he wishes to know its characteristics, how one can tell a good specimen from a bad one, how a reputable breeder operates a breeding program, advice on purchasing a puppy, its feeding and care through adulthood, training, showing in breed and obedience competition, coursing, and hunting. He will also be interested in literature on the subject and in the pronunciation of Irish names. The Contents table will show that this is the order that has been followed. If the reader has just purchased a puppy or is going to do so before he can read this entire book, I recommend that he give priority to Chapters IV (Sections A, B), V, and then III.

Acknowledgement is made of the contributions of persons and organizations who authorized reproduction of copyrighted material: Stephen J. Field, Gaines Nutrition Center, Frederick B. Hutt, Irish Wolfhound Club of America, Inc., Popular Dogs, and Ralston Purina Company.

Miss Máirín Ní Dhomhnallaín, Assistant Librarian, Royal Irish Academy, Dublin, has given an authoritative stamp to the pronunciation of Irish names and words which persons might find useful in naming their hounds or in pronouncing the names of those already named.

The work involved in obtaining photographic evidence of qualities and faults in dogs is considerable. Credit for accomplishment is due to Fredrick and Nanse Schlexer ("Duncairn") who were called upon, first to evaluate the Irish Wolfhounds they saw, then to have them photographed. The excellent photographic results are mostly the handiwork of Miss Marty Ackerman and of Boardman Moore ("Bally Mor") with the

cooperation of Jessie and Newell Kelley ("Kelley's Glen"). Nanse, whose artistic talents extend to painting, sculpture and poetry, also produced all the sketches which supplement the photographs and is responsible for the detailed photographs on grooming taken by Martha Ackerman. The many other persons who contributed individual photographs are mentioned in the section captioned "Illustrations."

The generous and cordial support received from the staff of the Library of Congress is appreciated: Steven Hernan, Chief of the Stack and Reader Division; his assistant, William Sartain; Ann Helstein, Head of the Reader Services Section and John F. Thomas, her assistant.

                                             ALFRED W. DeQUOY
6800 Broyhill Street
McLean, Virginia 22101

Contents

I. HISTORY 1

II. CHARACTERISTICS 4

III. STANDARD OF EXCELLENCE 21

IV. THE BREEDER'S RESPONSIBILITIES
    A. General 75
    B. Breeding Objectives 78
    C. Genetics 97
    D. Premating Considerations 113
    E. Mating 118
    F. Gestation Period 122
    G. Whelping 127
    H. Postwhelping Considerations 132
    I. Weaning 143

V. THE PUPPY
    A. Sales 149
    B. Care 170
    C. Feeding 181

VI. THE ADULT HOUND
    A. Feeding 188
    B. Care 202
    C. Health Maintenance 217
    D. First Aid 235

VII. OBEDIENCE
    A. Training 243
    B. Showing 254

VIII. BREED COMPETITION
    A. General 261
    B. Grooming 263
    C. Preparations 266
    D. Showing 271
    E. Foreign Shows 278

IX. COURSING AND TRACKING 282

X. HUNTING 304

APPENDIX

A.   Report of World Small Animal Veterinary Association   332

B.   Registrations   342

C.   Irish Wolfhound Literature

    1. Non-Fiction
      (a) Current   346
      (b) Out of Print   347
    2. Fiction   348

D.   Irish Names

    1. Pronunciation Guide   349
    2. Names of Men   350
    3. Names of Women   351
    4. Family Names   352
    5. Irish Wolfhound Names Mentioned in
      Irish Literature   354
    6. Miscellaneous   358

Bibliography

    Documents Cited   362
    Other Documents Consulted   369

Index   370

Illustrations

Frontispiece

Color. Keltic Siobhan, C.D., Ch. Keltic Findabair, Ch. Ballykelly Charlie Girl, C.D., Ch. Sulhamstead Marda, C.D.

Between pages 32 and 33

1. *Irish Greyhound* by P. Reinagle (1803).
2. Ard Ri of Ballylyke, C.D., and Ch. Feasgar Bruadar of Ballylyke, U.D., with owner Alfred W. DeQuoy (1959).
3. Major Acres Tancred O'Magnus, C.D. (1977).
4. Ch. Keltic Tara, C.D.X., Ch. Keltic Banshee, U.D., Ch. Keltic Phantom II, C.D.X., Ch. Sulhamstead Samando Patrick, C.D. (1966).

Pages 39 and 43

5. Mean height and weight of North American Irish Wolfhounds. Graph.
6. Mean height of North American and Ambleside Irish Wolfhounds. Graph.
7. Mean weight of North American and Ambleside Irish Wolfhounds. Graph.

Between pages 48 and 49

8. Standard of Excellence. Ch. Clodagh of Ouborough (1925).
9. External parts of the Irish Wolfhound. Ch. Felixstowe Kilmorac Halcyon (1930).
10. Skeletal parts of the Irish Wolfhound. Sketch.
11. Skeletons of dog, horse and man.
12. Scot (1879).
13. Ch. Sulhamstead Melba (1963).
14. Ch. Wild Isle Warlock with owner Mrs. Louis Bregy (1974).

15. Ch. Kihone Mearose of Cu with owner Miss F. Jeannette McGregor (1973).

16. Scottish Deerhound Ch. Lyonhils Highland Fortune with owner Mrs. Fredrick Schlexer.

17. Greyhound Ch. Fawnglen's Fascination with handler Mrs. Fredrick Schlexer.

18. Great Dane.

19. Chulainn Dauntless (1926).

20. Ballymor Ajax and Christine Moore. Illustration of comparative heights were the Irish Wolfhound four feet tall (1977).

21. Ambleside Finn of Erinn with owner Alma Starbuck.

22. Ch. Fuath of Ulaid (1960).

23. Ch. Ballykelly Dalkey (1971).

24. Well-proportioned head.

25. Short muzzle.

26. Flat ears.

27. Broad muzzle.

28. Head study in color. Ch. Kihone Mearose of Cu (1973). Pastel on velour.

29. Color. Light eyes.

30. Color. Blue eyes.

31. Measurement of scapular angle.

32. Measurement of scapular angle. Close-up.

33. Ch. Keltic Findabair being measured by Glenna and Alfred de Quoy (1971).

34. Level bite.

35. Scissors bite.

36. Overshot. Appearance of teeth.

37. Overshot. Appearance of muzzle.

38. Undershot. Appearance of teeth.

39. Undershot. Appearance of muzzle.

40. Good front.

41. Out at elbows.

42. Narrow front.

43. Broad front. Splay feet.

44. Irish Wolfhound with Scottish Deerhound appearance.

45. Flat feet.

46. Side view of good forequarters.

47. Shallow chest. Feet turned out. Light bone.

48. Sloping top line.

49. Hollow back.

50. Roached back.

51. Back too straight.

52. Good rear angulation. Side view of Keltic Siobhan, C.D.

53. Insufficient rear angulation.

54. Rear over-angulated.

55. Weak thighs.

56. Good rear angulation. Rear view of Keltic Siobhan, C.D.

57. "Cowhocks"

58. Sacrum too flat.

59. Tail used for balance.

60. Ch. Fleetwind Roise of Ronor, F. Ch., coursing.

61. Ch. Sanctuary Fair Erin, F. Ch., coursing.

62. Long coat.

63. Clipped soft coat.

64. Sheelah (1890)

Pages 57, 63, 67, 105

65. Measurement of scapular angle. Sketches.

66. Tail carriage. Sketches.

67. Movement. Sketches.

68. Probability of colors in dogs. Matrix.

Between pages 130 and 131

69. Whelping pen.

70. Keltic Siobhan, C.D. Fifteen minutes old (1971).

71. Ch. Sulhamstead Marda, C.D., Ch. Ballykelly Charlie Girl, C.D., and four-week-old Keltic Siobhan, C.D. (1971).

72. Litter of five-week-old puppies (1925).

73. Ch. High and Mighty of Carrickmines and Ch. Ballykelly Powerscourt Tomas at three months (1968).

74. Inisfail Kate at three months (1977).

Between pages 146 and 147

75. Gavage. Marking the tube.

76. Gavage. Inserting the tube.

77. Major Acres Tancred O'Magnus, C.D., at 6 months (1977).

78. Major Acres "S" of Engerth (1977).

79. Major Acres Rial Dhu, C.D., at 11 weeks (1977).

Between pages 162 and 163

80. Two five-month-old puppies (1940).

81. Ch. Gweebarra of Eagle at 7½ months (1971). Breeder-owner-handler Samuel E. Ewing, III. Judge Alfred W. DeQuoy.

Between pages 178 and 179

82. Major Acres Rial Dhu, C.D., at 11 weeks (1977).

83. Ch. Keltic Findabair leaving the house by a two-way swinging door (1972).

84. Year-old Keltic Carragan and his litter sister, Keltic Aluinn, at play (1977).

Pages 186 and 201

85. Mean weight of puppies. Graph.

86. Nutrient comparisons. Chart.

Between pages 250 and 251

87. Correct way of putting a chain collar on a dog. Keltic Dathchaoin with Mrs. Alfred DeQuoy (1977).

88. Collars and clasps.

89. Ch. Feasgar Bruadar of Ballylyke, U.D., clearing a 3-foot single bar jump (1957).

90. Marhaba of Berryfield, W.D. Ex., U.D. Ex., T.D. Ex., scaling a 6-foot wall (1977).

91. Marhaba of Berryfield at the top of the wall (1977).

92. R. Montagu Scott exercising his hounds (1925).

93. Breaking cover. Hounds of R. Montagu Scott (1925).

94. Dan O'Malley of Ambleside with his owner, Desmond Slattery (1953).

95. Kevin Kilkelly of Skyline and Palomino Kelly of Skyline with owner, James G. Haizlip.

96. Gael Pendragon of Eagle gnawing a shoe.

97. Gael Pendragon of Eagle looking at torn paper.

98. Gael Pendragon of Eagle digging.

99. Gael Pendragon of Eagle leaning on a bed.

100. Major Acres Tancred O'Magnus and Major Acres Rial Dhu, C.D.

101. H.M. The Queen and Shaun (1966).

Between pages 274 and 275

102–
125. Grooming. Ch. Malachi McCourt of Dundrum (1977).

126. Ch. Siobhan O'Born of Erinmore at 5 months (1970).

127. Roddy of Killybracken with Mary Jane Ellis (1976).

128. Team. Ch. Keltic Phantom II, C.D.X., Ch. Keltic Banshee, U.D., Ch. Keltic Ghost of Ballylyke, C.D., Ch. Keltic Tara, C.D.X. With the author, breeder-owner-handler. Judge Winifred Heckmann.

129. Effect of posing a hound with hind feet too far apart. Keltic Siobhan, C.D.

130. Effect of posing a hound with hind feet too close together. Keltic Siobhan, C.D.

Between pages 298 and 299

131.   Irish Wolfhounds pursuing a hare.

132.   Ch. Sulhamstead Match (1971).

133.   Mixed field in pursuit of a hare: Whippet, Saluki, two Grey-
hounds, Ch. Keystone's Garda Siocana Doc, Ch. Keystone's
Lace Curtain Irish, Ch. Keystone's Gretchen and Keystone's
Sage of Kingarrow.

134.   Marhaba of Berryfield, W.D. Ex., U.D. Ex., T.D. Ex., in a
tracking test in England.

135.   Michael John Bowen with his Ch. Sanctuary Fair Erin,
F. Ch.; Janet McEwan with her Ch. Dannybrook Jason,
F. Ch.; Dr. Jack England with Mr. Bowen's Ch. Kilchrohane
Sandra, F. Ch. at 1977 Grand National Lure Course.

136.   Ch. Sanctuary Fair Erin, F. Ch., released by owner, Michael
John Bowen.

Between pages 306 and 307

137.   Ch. Feasgar Bruadar of Ballylyke, U.D., side by side with
stuffed Wyoming wolf (1957).

138.   Ch. Feasgar Bruadar of Ballylyke, U.D., facing stuffed
Wyoming wolf (1957).

Between pages 322 and 323

139.   Ch. Aran of Kileen, the wolf he killed, and Doria Francis
(1972).

140.   Ch. Sabre of Norwolf.

Page 345

141.   Registrations. Graph.

Credits

Ackerman, Martha — 24, 26, 27, 40, 45-48, 50, 54, 55, 57, 74, 102-124
Armstrong, Peter — 133
Ashbey, John L. — 53, 127
Booth, Martin — 14, 52, 56
Curtis, Jack — 132
Francis, Robert — 139
Francisco, Molly — 28
Gaines Dog Research Progress — 8
Gilbert, William P. — 18, 81
Hanophy, Teddie — 96-99
Hewett, Richard — 97
Huntley, Patricia — 29, 30, 51
Kelleher, Arthur J. — 15
Kelley, Jessie and Newell — 35, 49, 58
Mahood, William — 140
Moore, Boardman — 3, 20, 31, 32, 34, 38, 39, 63, 77-79, 82, 100
Murphy, Elizabeth — 23
Murphy, Joseph — 62
Northcott, Eugene and Royce — 59, 60
Schlexer, Nanse — 10, 65-67, 125
Stacks, Richard — 22

From foreground: Red fawn (Keltic Siobhan, C.D.), red wheaten (Ch. Keltic Findabair, C.D.), red (Ch. Ballykelly Charlie Girl, C.D.), grey brindle (Ch. Sulhamstead Marda, C.D.).